I Wonder, I Wonder

TEXT/By Marguerite Kurth Frey   EDITOR/W. J. Fields

ART/Concordia Films

Concordia

Publishing House
St. Louis   London

Parents to Be

Eight-year-old John tumbled out of bed. He dressed with flying fingers. "Mother and our twin babies are coming home from the hospital today," he shouted to his sister Julia.

Julia wriggled under her blankets and made waking-up sounds. "Is it Saturday?" she asked and crawled out of bed. She crossed the room and pressed her sleepy 6-year-old face against the window to look at the June morning.

"Hurry up, you slowpoke," John called from down the hall as he brushed his teeth. Julia

Concordia Publishing House, St. Louis, Missouri
Concordia Publishing House Ltd., London, E. C.
© 1967 by Concordia Publishing House
Library of Congress Catalog Card No. 67-24879
MANUFACTURED IN THE UNITED STATES OF AMER

went to her closet, put on a dress, and then hunted about the floor until she found an old pair of her mother's high-heeled shoes.

Julia joined John. "I'll be a mother when I grow up," she told him. John gurgled through the foamy toothpaste.

"And you'll be a father," said Julia.

"Yes, just like Daddy," said John. He ran down the hall to the kitchen. Julia ran after him, her high heels clattering and chattering on the floor.

Grandma was pulling a crusty, hot apple pie from the oven. "Mmmmmmm," said John as he ran round and round her. "I'll miss your pies when you go home again."

Julia flew into the kitchen. "Grandma, I'm going to be a mother when I grow up. See my high heels."

Grandma laughed. "You certainly will, Julia. But it takes more than high heels to make a mother."

"What does it take, Grandma?" asked Julia.

Many Things Make a Mother

Grandma said, "Many things make a mother. Help me name some of them."

"A mother has to know how to make apple pie," piped up Julia.

"That's part of it," said Grandma.

"And a mother mends holes when they

start," said Daddy as he came into the kitchen for breakfast. He sniffed the sweet-smelling pie.

"Mother puts a bandage on where I hurt and dries my tears," said John. "And she tucks me in at night and says my prayers with me."

"A mother is soft and warm and has a nice lap. And when I tell her something, she listens to me," said Julia.

John was excited. He waved his arms. "You forgot the most important thing. A woman has to have a baby before she's a mother."

Daddy smiled. "Of course. And before that a man and woman love each other and marry and together make a family that God will bless."

Many Things Make a Father

"Let's name the things that make a father," Julia said.

"Daddy works almost every day so we'll have food to eat and warm clothes and a warm house in winter," said John.

Grandma said, "God has made a father the head of his household, sort of like its chief. He loves you and Mother and protects you."

"And he makes up funny stories to tell us,"

said Julia. "He throws us up in the air and kisses us goodnight. That's what I like best about my Daddy."

What Makes a Baby?

"But what makes a baby?" asked John.

Daddy said, "With God's help a man and woman make a baby, a man and woman who love each other."

"Is that when they get married and every-one throws rice at them?" asked Julia.

"When a man and woman love each other, they usually get married, and then they have God's blessing to start a family. Your Mother and Dad loved each other and got married."

"Then I was born," said John. "And Julia."

"And now we have the twins," said Julia. "Our family got much bigger all of a sudden."

"We'd better get ready for our bigger family," Daddy said. "Help me get your old crib out of the garage. It will be for Baby Sam, and it needs a slat fixed on it. Baby Sue's new crib is already in their room."

After breakfast John, Julia, and Daddy moved the old crib onto a patch of grass in the sun. "Where did the twins come from?" asked Julia. "They weren't here last week, and now all of a sudden they're here. Where were they?"

"They were here last week, but you didn't see them," said John. "They were growing inside Mother."

Julia laughed. "Were they playing hide-and-go-seek with us?"

"They weren't hiding on purpose, you imp," Daddy said. "It just wasn't time for them to be born yet."

"How did they get out of Mother?" asked John.

"I don't see how they ever got inside her," said Julia.

God's Plan

"Whoa there, both of you," said Daddy. "Sit down, and let me tell you the story of how and why you got here."

Daddy sat down in the shade. John and Julia

curled up next to him. "Every child needs to be born into a family. He needs a family to love him, kiss him, talk to him, feed him. He needs many things done for him when he's small."

"Sam and Sue can't even sit up or walk or talk," said John.

"A brand-new baby can just about lift his head up. He can't even see clearly. He needs his mother and father, his family, to stay alive. The family is God's way of giving a child a happy growing-up place."

Growing Up

"When the twins are older, they'll learn to sit up, then crawl and walk and talk," said Daddy.

"I can tie my shoes now," said Julia.

"And I can make my own bed now," said John.

"That's all part of learning to grow up. Puppies and kittens grow up very fast; just a year or so, and they're dogs and cats already. But a human child needs long years." Daddy put his arms around Julia and John. "When you're all grown up, you can take care of yourselves completely."

"Can I be a father then?" asked John.

"Yes, then you can. And Julia can be a mother. God lets us share in His creation. Creation means making something new. You'll help God in making new people."

"Tell us how the twins were made inside Mother's stomach," John said.

"They weren't made in her stomach — where our food goes when we swallow — although many children think that's the place where babies grow."

"Where is the place?" asked John.

The Uterus

"Inside every mother is a special baby-growing place. It has different names like womb or uterus. You're old enough now to call it by the grown-up name of uterus," said Daddy.

"You-ter-us," said Julia, slowly. "It's not hard to say."

"What does it look like? A crib?" asked John.

"The uterus is shaped like a balloon with a little air blown into it." Daddy scratched a picture of it on the ground with a twig. "The walls are thicker though and are made of muscle. The walls stretch and the uterus gets big when a baby is growing in it. When the baby leaves, the walls shrink down again."

"Where does the baby get out of the uterus?" asked John.

"The uterus has an opening that looks pretty much like the opening at the bottom of a balloon. The baby leaves through this opening when it's all finished growing."

A Baby Starts as a Tiny Speck

"But how did the twins start inside the uterus?" Julia asked.

"Each baby started from tiny, tiny parts of Mother

and me. That's why you and John and the twins, Sue and Sam, look like us. You're really tiny parts of us that have grown big," said Daddy.

"What tiny parts? Where are they?" asked John.

Mother's Egg

"The tiny part of a mother that helps start a baby is called her egg," said Daddy. "Every mother has eggs inside her near the uterus. The tiny part of the father that helps start a baby is called his sperm."

"Does a mother have an egg in her like a hen?" asked John.

Daddy rumpled John's hair. "Not as big as a hen's egg. Not even as big as a raisin. Think of the smallest thing that you can see."

"Small as an ant's eye?" asked John.

"Yes, I think an ant's eye can hardly be seen."

"Or a mosquito's footprint," said Julia.

Daddy laughed. "If he walked in ink and then left a footprint on a white piece of paper, it would be about the right size. Or think of the smallest piece of sand you can rub between your fingers and still feel it."

"I'm surprised I'm here if I started out that small," said John.

Daddy's Sperm

"Wait, John. You're going to be even more surprised. The father's sperm is ever so much smaller than the mother's egg. It can't even be seen by the human eye. It's just as important though. Only when the father's sperm joins the mother's egg can a baby start." Daddy scratched again in the dirt with his twig. "Here, I'll draw a picture of a mother's egg and

a father's sperm. The sperm has a little head and a long, long, tail."

"Where does a man have his sperm, Daddy?" asked John.

"The sperm are in the bag or sack that hangs between a man's legs. It's called the scro-tum."

"Scro-tum," said John. "That's easy to say."

While they were talking Grandma came from the house with a pan of hot, soapy water. She gave Julia a cloth, and together they splashed and dashed water on the crib. Then they rubbed and scrubbed it. Daddy and John fixed the broken slat.

Soon the crib was sparkling clean. Julia and Grandma polished it with wax until it shone in the sun. Grandma stood back and looked at it. "Now we're ready for the new babies in our family." John and Julia turned somersaults on the grass. Then everyone helped to carry the crib into the house and set it down gently in the twins' room.

Nine Months to Make a Baby

Then John asked, "How long does it take for that tiny speck to grow into a baby?"

"It takes nine months for the tiny speck

that is the egg and sperm joined to grow into a baby in the uterus," Daddy said.

"Is nine months a long time?" asked Julia.

"It's the same time it took you to go through Kindergarten, Julia. The twins started growing in Mother's uterus last fall when the leaves were turning yellow. Remember? You just started school then. The babies grew all winter and spring."

"That's the same time it took me to go through second grade," said John.

How a Baby Grows Inside a Mother

"It must be magic how that tiny speck grows big into a baby," said Julia. "I don't see how it can happen."

"It's God's magic," Daddy said. "Let's go to the kitchen while Grandma fixes lunch, and I'll show you how a baby grows." Daddy took a paper napkin, sat down at the kitchen table, and drew pictures on it. "Here is the tiny speck that was Daddy's sperm and Mother's egg. If you had magic eyes, you could see it big, like this. Now the speck divides in half, just splits down the middle, the way Grandma is cutting her apple pie in half now." John and Julia crowded close to Daddy to see.

"Now there are two pieces. These two pieces grow and then they divide in half, and poof! there are four pieces. This goes on and soon there is a living ball of cells, which is what the pieces are called. This tiny ball, the beginning baby, settles down in the thick lining of the uterus, where it gets lots of food and keeps growing until it is a big baby."

"Did Mother know the twins were inside her?" asked Julia.

"At first they were so small Mother hardly knew they were there. Then when they had been growing in her about four months, she felt a light tapping from inside."

"That was Sue and Sam tapping," Julia said.

"Yes, they were stretching their feet and moving their arms about. It was as if they said, 'Hello, we're here.'"

"And when they got bigger, they made Mother stick out in front," John said.

"They had to have room to grow, and since there are no bones towards the front of the lower body, they leaned that way," Daddy said. "When Sam was born, he was as long as from my elbow to my fingertips and weighed a little more than a 5-pound bag of sugar." Grandma reached

to a shelf and brought down a 5-pound bag of sugar for Julia and John to hold.

"Sue weighed a little less," Daddy said. "Girls usually don't weigh as much as boys when they're born."

The Twins Come Home

After lunch Daddy left to bring the twins and Mother home from the hospital. John and Julia sat on the front steps of their home and waited and yawned and waited some more. "They're taking a terribly long time to get home," said Julia.

"Daddy said I could carry Mother's suitcase to the house," said John.

"And I'll carry something for the twins," Julia said.

Soon their car came up the street. John and Julia ran to meet it. They kissed Mother and hugged her. "It's good to see you two again. Look in the back seat at your new brother and sister." John and Julia peeked at two red faces and brown tufts of hair all but buried in blankets.

"They don't look very pretty," said John.

"They'll improve with age, you'll see," said Daddy.

In a few minutes the twins were in their cribs in their new nursery. "They wiggle more than my dolls do," said Julia as she watched Sue and Sam stretch.

Mother Gives Baby Milk and Love

All through the afternoon the twins slept. John and Julia walked past their room many times hoping they would wake up. At 4 o'clock Sam squirmed. Then he gave a short cry. John ran to Mother. "Do something, Sam's crying."

"He's hungry. It's time for me to feed him."

"Grandma says you'll feed the babies from your breasts. They have milk in them now," said Julia.

"Yes, God gave mothers breasts to feed their babies with. You saw our mother cat feed her kittens from her breasts. When a mother holds her baby close to her when feeding him, he feels someone loves him and he's happy."

Grandma heard Sam too. She carried him to Mother. Mother soon had Sam settled down and drinking warm milk.

"Do all mothers feed their babies from their breasts?" asked Julia.

"Some mothers feed their babies from bottles. They grow up strong and contented too. The mother holds the baby close and snug to her when she feeds him, so he gets that same happy, loving feeling."

How Baby Was Fed Inside Mother

Mother held Sam to her shoulder when he finished eating. She patted him on the back. He blinked and burped. John and Julia laughed.

"What did Sam eat when he was inside you, Mother?" asked Julia. "Did he have a hose going to your stomach?"

"He did have a hollow tube called a cord, Julia. But it didn't go to my stomach. It went from the middle of his tummy to the wall of my uterus. The cord carried good air and food in very small pieces from my body to his."

"Where is his cord now?" asked John.

"After he was born, he didn't need it anymore, so it dropped off. He now breathes his own air and eats with his mouth. You can see the round scar the cord made in your middle too."

"We call it our belly button," said John.

"I know," said Mother. "I did too when I was a girl. In a way it does look like a button. Now we call it a navel."

How Baby Gets Out of the Uterus

"How did Sue and Sam get out of your uterus?" asked John.

"After 9 months Sue and Sam were finished babies and ready to live in air instead of the bag of water they had been floating in. Sam was first to leave the uterus. He slowly pushed out headfirst through the opening at the bottom of the uterus and then to the outside. It was then that he took his first breath and had his first cry."

"Did Sam just fall out on his head, Mother?" Julia asked.

Mother laughed. "No, that would never do. I was lying on a table in the hospital in a special clean room where babies are born. The doctor helped him out and then gave him to a nurse who weighed him. Then she laid him down in a little crib in the hospital nursery. By the time Sam was in his first clothes, Sue had come out too, in the same way."

A Prayer for the Twins

At supper that evening Daddy said, "We'll say a different prayer tonight." John and Julia folded their hands.

"Thank You, Lord Jesus, for bringing Mother and Sam and Sue home safely to us. May they grow up to be a boy and girl You will be proud of. We hope they'll follow in the footsteps You took with Your mother and father in Palestine two thousand years ago. May their beautiful young minds and bodies always do the things that please You. Amen."

The Twins' Bath

Early the next morning John and Julia crowded close to the table where Mother was bathing Sue and Sam. "Ladies first," said Mother as she lifted Sue to the warm towel on the table. She dipped the washcloth into a pan of warm water. Gently she wiped Sue's head and face. Sue shut her eyes and squealed in surprise.

"Why don't you just put her in the water?" asked Julia.

"Brand-new babies aren't quite ready for a

real bath like older babies. Her navel shouldn't get wet yet." Mother washed Sue's round, pink bottom. She turned her over.

"Girls sure are different from boys," said John.

"God made them different so each could do the work He planned for them." Mother washed Sue gently.

"Does Sue have a place for babies to come out of?" asked Julia.

"Yes. All girls do. Between the opening where the waste water comes out and the opening for waste solids is the opening through which babies are born."

A Boy's Parts

"Sam's turn," said Mother. She laid Sue back in her crib and picked Sam up. He kicked his feet on the table and wriggled as Mother washed him.

"Sam has a scrotum too, Mom," said John.

"Yes, all boys do. And all boys have a penis, which is the grown-up name for the part above the scrotum that sort of looks like a finger. The waste water comes out through the penis, and at different times the sperm does when a boy becomes a man."

Grandma came into the twins' room. "Sue and Sam are clean for Sunday," said Julia.

"So they are." Grandma chuckled at the two pink faces peeking out from their blankets. "Time for breakfast, John and Julia. Daddy is already getting dressed for church."

Children Are Gifts of God

At Sunday school an hour later John and Julia told their friends about the twins. "I think twins would be more a pain in the neck than a blessing from God," said one of John's classmates.

John told Daddy about this just before church started. Daddy laughed. "Let's listen to what our pastor says about that."

Julia and John sat with Daddy in church. Their ears perked up when they heard their minister say, "We give thanks this morning for the birth of Sue and Sam, whom the Lord brought safely to their parents. Let us pray for them." John and Julia bowed their heads and listened to the prayer.

When they reached home after church, John and Julia ran up the walk to their house. They found Grandma and Mother in the kitchen finishing dinner. "Mom, Sue and Sam had their own special prayer in church today," said Julia.

"And a friend of mine wasn't sure they were a blessing, but I think he was teasing me," said John. "Anyway, our minister said the twins were like a present from God."

"And he's right," Mother said. "All children are gifts from God. You too. That's why we love you so much."